Hallelujah, and praises to your name God.
Father today we stretch ourselves before you, in
total surrender to your will. As it is your desire
that we ought to communicate with you, teach
me how to pray and learn the importance of
prayer, that I might seek you daily. Give me the
pose and right positioning to be more effective in
prayer in Jesus name, Amen.

Table of Contents

Introduction

Definition of Virtue

Moral excellence or goodness (Phil 4:8). Virtue is considered a necessary ingredient in the exercise of faith (2 Peter 1:3,5). "**For His divine power has bestowed upon us all things that [are requisite and suited] to life and godliness, through the [full, personal] knowledge of Him Who called us by and to His own glory and excellence (virtue).**

2 Peter 1:5 "For this very reason, adding your diligence [to the divine promises], employ every effort in exercising your faith to develop virtue (excellence, resolution, Christian energy), and in [exercising] virtue [develop] knowledge (intelligence)."

Sometimes the Greek word for virtue is used to express the idea of power or strength (Luke 6:19).

Luke 6:19 "And all the multitude were seeking to touch Him, for healing power was all the while going forth from Him and curing them all [saving them from severe illnesses or calamities]."

Spiritual Nugget

Knowing where God is in a situation before praying is very important. It will help you on how and what to pray.

Prayer Nuggets

Matthew 18:19-20 "Again I tell you, if two of you on earth agree (harmonize together, make a symphony together) about whatever [anything and everything] they may ask, it will come to pass and be done for them by My Father in heaven. For wherever two or three are gathered (drawn together as My followers) in (into) My name, there I AM in the midst of them. [Exod. 3:14.]"

What is Prayer?

It's a dialogue between you and God. Prayer is communication with God. Not just the ability to speak to God, but also to hear from God in quietness after prayer.

1 Thessalonians 5:16 **Be happy [in your faith] and rejoice and be glad-hearted continually (always);**

1 Thessalonians 5:17 **Be unceasing in prayer [praying perseveringly];**

1 Thessalonians 5:18 **Thank [God] in everything [no matter what the circumstances may be, be thankful and give thanks], for this is the will of God for you [who are] in Christ Jesus [the Revealer and Mediator of that will].**

Prayer Nuggets

Mark 13:35 **"Therefore watch (give strict attention, be cautious and alert), for you do not know when the Master of the house is coming–in the evening, or at midnight, or at cockcrowing, or in the morning."**

The Standard of Prayer

We must understand that we cannot go before a Holy God dirty and unclean. So it is important to repent before God, asking Him to forgive us of our sins, and that we repent (turn away from those actions, asking Him for boldness to go forward and focusness not to return down that pathway again). After He has purged us, we are now in position to praise Him, praise Him for all that He has done in the past concerning family, friends and even yourself. Praise Him for His excellent works, praise for the work He is doing now, and praise for the works He will do in the future. Praise Him just for being God and the mighty works that He has performed. This now takes us to a position of worshiping.

Tell God who He is, what He means to us, recognizing who is of highest worth. Him being deserving of the highest worship and of the highest respect. Now you are in position to pray to our God the Father.

Prayer Nuggets

Luke 21:36 **"Keep awake then and watch at all times [be discreet, attentive, and ready], praying that you may have the full strength and ability and be accounted worthy to escape all these things [taken together] that will take place, and to stand in the presence of the Son of Man."**

Positioning in Prayer

It is always important to repent before God, for the things you have done knowingly and the things you know not of (you didn't recognize that you did).

Next: **praise God for who He is.** (sing praises)

Next: **worship the one true God.** Tell Him what he is to you. (also sing worship songs).

Next: **read the word of God.** Meditate on it (think about it and apply it to your life).

Now you are ready to pray.

<u>Different Types of Prayer</u>

Prayer of Thanksgiving

What is the meaning of thanksgiving?

The expression of gratitude, especially to God. I believe that this is a place in prayer to be thankful unto God for all that He has done. Even for the things that He has promised, as we have not seen yet, we should still be thankful unto to Him. Not just for what we can get, or for what has been promised, but because He is our God. Philippians 4:6 **"Do not fret or have any anxiety about anything, but in every circumstance and in everything, by prayer and petition (definite requests), with thanksgiving, continue to make your wants known to God."**

Prayer of Repentance

What is repentance?

A turning away from sin, disobedience or rebellion and a turning back to God. A feeling of remorse or regret for actions past or present. Matthew 27.

Matthew 27 **"When Judas, His betrayer, saw that [Jesus] was condemned, [Judas was afflicted in mind and troubled for his former folly; and] with remorse [with little more than a selfish dread of the consequences] he brought back the thirty pieces of silver to the chief priests and the elders, [Exod. 21:32.]"**

Spiritual Nugget

Genesis 20:7 **"So now restore to the man his wife, for he is a prophet, and he will pray for you and you will live. But if you do not restore her [to him], know that you shall surely die, you and all who are yours."** *The Lord commissioned King Abimelech to let the Prophet Abraham pray for him and he shall live.*

Another example of repentance Psalms 51

Psalm 51 To the Chief Musician. A Psalm of David; when Nathan the prophet came to him after he had sinned with Bathsheba.

Psalm 51:1 **"HAVE MERCY upon me, O God, according to Your steadfast love; according to the multitude of Your tender mercy and loving-kindness blot out my transgressions."**

11

Psalm 51:2 **"Wash me thoroughly [and repeatedly] from my iniquity and guilt and cleanse me and make me wholly pure from my sin!"**

Psalm 51:3 "**For I am conscious of my transgressions and I acknowledge them; my sin is ever before me.**"

Psalm 51:4 **"Against You, You only, have I sinned and done that which is evil in Your sight, so that You are justified in Your sentence and faultless in Your judgment. [Rom. 3:4.]"**

Psalm 51:5 **"Behold, I was brought forth in [a state of] iniquity; my mother was sinful who conceived me [and I too am sinful]. [John 3:6; Rom. 5:12; Eph. 2:3.]"**

Psalm 51:6 **"Behold, You desire truth in the inner being; make me therefore to know wisdom in my inmost heart."**

Psalm 51:7 **"Purify me with hyssop, and I shall be clean [ceremonially]; wash me, and I shall [in reality] be whiter than snow."**

Psalm 51:8 **"Make me to hear joy and gladness and be satisfied; let the bones which You have broken rejoice."**

Psalm 51:9 **"Hide Your face from my sins and blot out all my guilt and iniquities."**

Psalm 51:10 **"Create in me a clean heart, O God, and renew a right, persevering, and steadfast spirit within me."**

Psalm 51:11 **"Cast me not away from Your presence and take not Your Holy Spirit from me."**

Psalm 51:12 **"Restore to me the joy of Your salvation and uphold me with a willing spirit."**

Psalm 51:13 **"Then will I teach transgressors Your ways, and sinners shall be converted and return to You."**

Psalm 51:14 **"Deliver me from bloodguiltiness and death, O God, the God of my salvation, and my tongue shall sing aloud of Your righteousness (Your rightness and Your justice)."**

Psalm 51:15 "O Lord, open my lips, and my mouth shall show forth Your praise."

Psalm 51:16 "For You delight not in sacrifice, or else would I give it; You find no pleasure in burnt offering. [I Sam. 15:22.]"

Psalm 51:17 "My sacrifice [the sacrifice acceptable] to God is a broken spirit; a broken and a contrite heart [broken down with sorrow for sin and humbly and thoroughly penitent], such, O God, You will not despise."

Psalm 51:18 "Do good in Your good pleasure to Zion; rebuild the walls of Jerusalem."

Psalm 51:19 "Then will You delight in the sacrifices of righteousness, justice, and right, with burnt offering and whole burnt offering; then bullocks will be offered upon Your altar."

Prayer of Worship

What is worship?

What is of the highest worth, not one's self, family, government, pastor, others, but the most High God. Only the Most High God deserves our highest praise, worship and respect.

Acts 13:2 **"While they were worshiping the Lord and fasting, the Holy Spirit said, Separate now for Me Barnabas and Saul for the work to which I have called them."**

Acts 13:3 **"Then after fasting and praying, they put their hands on them and sent them away."**

Prayer of Faith

What is faith?

The most effective prayer comes from a heart that places it's trust in the Most High God.

God speaks to us through the word of God, being the Bible, and our way of speaking back to Him is by fully trusting, obeying and having the faith to believe that all things are possible through God.

Prayer Nuggets

Matthew 13:13 **"This is the reason that I speak to them in parables: because having the power of seeing, they do not see; and having the power of hearing, they do not hear, nor do they grasp and understand."**

Prayer of Agreement

Meaning of agreement?

The absence of incompatibility between two things; consistency. This type of prayer is for two or more persons that understand the situation at hand and are in agreement with the same answer, or want God to do the same thing concerning a matter etc. Acts 1:14 **"All of these with their minds in full agreement devoted themselves steadfastly to prayer, [waiting together] with the women and Mary the mother of Jesus, and with His brothers."**

Prayer of Request

Meaning of request?

An act of asking politely or formally for something. When we are in need it is always correct to ask the Father, put your request before him, and allow Him to do what pleases him. Philippians 4:6 **"Do not fret or have any anxiety about anything, but in every circumstance and in everything, by prayer and petition (definite requests), with thanksgiving, continue to make your wants known to God."**

Prayer of Intercession

Meaning of intercession?

Intercessors prayer is the act of praying to a deity on behalf of others. It is my belief, as a believer in Christ Jesus, we are to carry others in prayer. Not just praying for ourselves, but for others all over the world as the spirit leads. Whatever and whoever He shows us, at a particular time in prayer is actually in need of prayer (someone interceding on their behalf). When we go in prayer it shouldn't be about us, it should really be about what the Holy Spirit allows to flash before us in prayer. Examples are names, numbers, colors, messages, pictures of events, and also what is whispered in our hearing because the Holy Spirit is very aware of what others are going through. And really at times he will show us what is coming concerning others, sometimes celebration, danger, sickness, confusion, blessings etc. But only if you remain in position are you able to help others.

Spiritual Nugget

John 17:1 **"WHEN JESUS had spoken these things, He lifted up His eyes to heaven and said, Father, the hour has come. Glorify and exalt and honor and magnify Your Son, so that Your Son may glorify and extol and honor and magnify You."**

John 17:2 **"[Just as] You have granted Him power and authority over all flesh (all humankind), [now glorify Him] so that He may give eternal life to all whom You have given Him."**

John 17:3 **"And this is eternal life: [it means] to know (to perceive, recognize, become acquainted with, and understand) You, the only true and real God, and [likewise] to know Him, Jesus [as the] Christ (the Anointed One, the Messiah), Whom You have sent."**

John 17:4 **"I have glorified You down here on the earth by completing the work that You gave Me to do."**

John 17:5 **"And now, Father, glorify Me along with Yourself and restore Me to such majesty and honor in Your presence as I had with You before the world existed."**

John 17:6 **"I have manifested Your Name [I have revealed Your very Self, Your real Self] to the people whom You have given Me out of the world. They were Yours, and You gave them to Me, and they have obeyed and kept Your word."**

John 17:7 **"Now [at last] they know and understand that all You have given Me belongs to You [is really and truly Yours]."**

John 17:8 **"For the [uttered] words that You gave Me I have given them; and they have received and accepted [them] and have come to know positively and in reality [to believe with absolute assurance] that I came forth from Your presence, and they have believed and are convinced that You did send Me."**

John 17:9 **"I am praying for them. I am not praying (requesting) for the world, but for those You have given Me, for they belong to You."**

John 17:10 **"All [things that are] Mine are Yours, and all [things that are] Yours belong to Me; and I am glorified in (through) them. [They have done Me honor; in them My glory is achieved.]"**

John 17:11 "And [now] I am no more in the world, but these are [still] in the world, and I am coming to You. Holy Father, keep in Your Name [in the knowledge of Yourself] those whom You have given Me, that they may be one as We [are one]."

John 17:12 "While I was with them, I kept and preserved them in Your Name [in the knowledge and worship of You]. Those You have given Me I guarded and protected, and not one of them has perished or is lost except the son of perdition [Judas Iscariot— the one who is now doomed to destruction, destined to be lost], that the Scripture might be fulfilled. [Ps. 41:9; John 6:70.]"

John 17:13 "And now I am coming to You; I say these things while I am still in the world, so that My joy may be made full and complete and perfect in them [that they may experience My delight fulfilled in them, that My enjoyment may be perfected in their own souls, that they may have My gladness within them, filling their hearts]."

John 17:14 "I have given and delivered to them Your word (message) and the world has hated them, because they are not of the world [do not belong to the world], just as I am not of the world."

John 17:15 **"I do not ask that You will take them out of the world, but that You will keep and protect them from the evil one."**

John 17:16 **"They are not of the world (worldly, belonging to the world), [just] as I am not of the world."**

John 17:17 **"Sanctify them [purify, consecrate, separate them for Yourself, make them holy] by the Truth; Your Word is Truth."**

John 17:18 **"Just as You sent Me into the world, I also have sent them into the world."**

John 17:19 **"And so for their sake and on their behalf I sanctify (dedicate, consecrate) Myself, that they also may be sanctified (dedicated, consecrated, made holy) in the Truth."**

John 17:20 **"Neither for these alone do I pray [it is not for their sake only that I make this request], but also for all those who will ever come to believe in (trust in, cling to, rely on) Me through their word and teaching,"**

John 17:21 **"That they all may be one, [just] as You, Father, are in Me and I in You, that they also may be one in Us, so that the world may believe and be convinced that You have sent Me."**

John 17:22 "I have given to them the glory and honor which You have given Me, that they may be one [even] as We are one:"

John 17:23 "I in them and You in Me, in order that they may become one and perfectly united, that the world may know and [definitely] recognize that You sent Me and that You have loved them [even] as You have loved Me".

John 17:24 "Father, I desire that they also whom You have entrusted to Me [as Your gift to Me] may be with Me where I am, so that they may see My glory, which You have given Me [Your love gift to Me]; for You loved Me before the foundation of the world."

John 17:25 "O just and righteous Father, although the world has not known You and has failed to recognize You and has never acknowledged You, I have known You [continually]; and these men understand and know that You have sent Me."

John 17:26 "I have made Your Name known to them and revealed Your character and Your very Self, and I will continue to make [You] known, that the love which You have bestowed upon Me may be in them [felt in their hearts] and that I [Myself] may be in them."

What Prayer Does?

It is my belief that prayer has power over everything that this world has to offer. Prayer has no boundaries or limits. There is no distance that prayer cannot reach. I am reminded of Matthew 8:5-13.

Matthew 8:5 **"As Jesus went into Capernaum, a centurion came up to Him, begging Him,".**

Matthew 8:6 **"And saying, Lord, my servant boy is lying at the house paralyzed and distressed with intense pains."**

Matthew 8:7 **"And Jesus said to him, I will come and restore him."**

Matthew 8:8 **"But the centurion replied to Him, Lord, I am not worthy or fit to have You come under my roof; but only speak the word, and my servant boy will be cured."**

Matthew 8:9 **"For I also am a man subject to authority, with soldiers subject to me. And I say to one, Go, and he goes; and to another, Come, and he comes; and to my slave, Do this, and he does it."**

Matthew 8:10 **"When Jesus heard him, He marveled and said to those who followed Him [who adhered steadfastly to Him, conforming to His example in living and, if need be, in dying also], I tell you truly, I have not found so much faith as this with anyone, even in Israel."**

Matthew 8:11 **"I tell you, many will come from east and west, and will sit at table with Abraham, Isaac, and Jacob in the kingdom of heaven,"**

Matthew 8:12 **"While the sons and heirs of the kingdom will be driven out into the darkness outside, where there will be weeping and grinding of teeth. [Ps. 107:2, 3; Isa. 49:12; 59:19; Mal. 1:11.]"**

Matthew 8:13 **"Then to the centurion Jesus said, Go; it shall be done for you as you have believed. And the servant boy was restored to health at that very moment."** (Here the centurion man asked Jesus to pray for his servant. The centurion said to Jesus just say the word because He understood that Jesus had authority, and him praying would have reached the distance and situations would have changed. This is exactly what happened.) Prayer changes things. Prayer cannot be stopped by mankind.

Hezekiah prayed a fervent prayer because two kings sent him a letter bashing his God and him. He prayed and an angel of the Lord killed 185,000 men quickly.

Isaiah 37:1 **"AND WHEN King Hezekiah heard it, he tore his clothes and covered himself with sackcloth and went into the house of the Lord. [II Kings 19:1-13.]"**

Isaiah 37:2 **"And he sent Eliakim, who was over the [royal] household, and Shebna the secretary, and the older priests, clothed with sackcloth, to Isaiah the prophet, the son of Amoz."**

Isaiah 37:3 **"And they said to him, Thus says Hezekiah: This day is a day of trouble and distress and of rebuke and of disgrace; for children have come to the birth, and there is no strength to bring them forth."**

Isaiah 37:4 **"It may be that the Lord your God will hear the words of the Rabshakeh, whom the king of Assyria, his master, has sent to mock, reproach, insult, and defy the living God, and will rebuke the words which the Lord your God has heard. Therefore lift up your prayer for the remnant [of His people] that is left."**

Isaiah 37:5 **"So the servants of King Hezekiah came to Isaiah."**

Isaiah 37:6 **"And Isaiah said to them, You shall say to your master, Thus says the Lord: Do not be afraid because of the words which you have heard, with which the servants of the king of Assyria have reviled and blasphemed Me."**

Isaiah 37:7 **"Behold, I will put a spirit in him so that he will hear a rumor and return to his own land, and I will cause him to fall by the sword in his own land."**

Isaiah 37:8 **"So the Rabshakeh returned and found the king of Assyria fighting against Libnah [a fortified city of Judah]; for he had heard that the king had departed from Lachish."**

Isaiah 37:9 **"And [Sennacherib king of Assyria] heard concerning Tirhakah king of Ethiopia, He has come forth to make war with you. And when he heard it, he sent messengers to Hezekiah, saying,"**

Isaiah 37:10 **"Thus shall you speak to Hezekiah king of Judah: Let not your God in Whom you trust deceive you by saying, Jerusalem shall not be given into the hand of the king of Assyria."**

Isaiah 37:11 **"Behold, you have heard what the kings of Assyria have done to all lands, destroying them utterly. And shall you be delivered?"**

Isaiah 37:12 **"Have the gods of the nations delivered those whom my predecessors have destroyed, as Gozan, Haran [of Mesopotamia], Rezeph, and the children of Eden who were in Telassar?"**

Isaiah 37:13 **"Where is the king of Hamath, and the king of Arpad [of northern Syria], and the king of the city of Sepharvaim, the king of Hena, or the king of Ivvah?"**

Isaiah 37:14 **"And Hezekiah received the letter from the hand of the messengers and read it. And Hezekiah went up to the house of the Lord and spread it before the Lord. [II Kings 19:14-19.]"**

Isaiah 37:15 **"And Hezekiah prayed to the Lord:"**

Isaiah 37:16 **"O Lord of hosts, God of Israel, Who [in symbol] are enthroned above the cherubim [of the ark in the temple], You are the God, You alone, of all the kingdoms of the earth. You have made heaven and earth."**

Isaiah 37:17 **"Incline Your ear, O Lord, and hear; open Your eyes, O Lord, and see; and hear all the words of Sennacherib which he has sent to mock, reproach, insult, and defy the living God."**

Isaiah 37:18 **"It is true, Lord, that the kings of Assyria have laid waste all the nations and their lands"**

Isaiah 37:19 **"And have cast the gods of those peoples into the fire, for they were not gods but the work of men's hands, wood and stone. Therefore they have destroyed them."**

Isaiah 37:20 **"Now therefore, O Lord our God, save us from his hand, that all the kingdoms of the earth may know (understand and realize) that You are the Lord, even You only."**

Isaiah 37:21 **"Then Isaiah son of Amoz sent to Hezekiah, saying, Thus says the Lord, the God of Israel: Because you have prayed to Me against Sennacherib king of Assyria, [II Kings 19:20-37; II Chron. 32:20-21.]"**

Isaiah 37:22 **"This is the word which the Lord has spoken concerning him: The Virgin Daughter of Zion has despised you and laughed you to scorn; the Daughter of Jerusalem has shaken her head behind you."**

Isaiah 37:23 **"Whom have you mocked and reviled [insulted and blasphemed]? And against Whom have you raised your voice and haughtily lifted your eyes? Against the Holy One of Israel!"**

Isaiah 37:24 **"By your servants you have mocked, reproached, insulted, and defied the Lord, and you have said, With my many chariots I have gone up to the height of the mountains, to the inner recesses of Lebanon. I cut down its tallest cedars and its choicest cypress trees; I came to its remotest height, its most luxuriant and dense forest;"**

Isaiah 37:25 "I dug wells and drank foreign waters, and with the sole of my feet I have dried up all the rivers [the Nile streams] of Egypt."

Isaiah 37:26 "[But, says the God of Israel] have you not heard that I planned to do it long ago, that I planned it in ancient times? Now I have brought it to pass, that you [king of Assyria] should [be My instrument to] lay waste fortified cities, making them ruinous heaps."

Isaiah 37:27 "Therefore their inhabitants had little power, they were dismayed and confounded; they were like the grass of the field and like the green herb, like the grass on the housetops and like a field of grain blasted before it is grown or is in stalk."

Isaiah 37:28 "But I [the Lord] know your sitting down and your going out and your coming in and your raging against Me."

Isaiah 37:29 "Because your raging against Me and your arrogance and careless ease have come to My ears, therefore will I put My hook in your nose and My bridle in your lips, and I will turn you back by the way you came."

Isaiah 37:30 "And [now, Hezekiah, says the Lord] this shall be the sign [of these things] to you: you shall eat this year what grows of itself, and in the second year that which springs from the same. And in the third year sow and reap, and plant vineyards and eat the fruit of them."

Isaiah 37:31 "And the remnant that has survived of the house of Judah shall again take root downward and bear fruit upward."

Isaiah 37:32 "For out of Jerusalem will go forth a remnant, and a band that survives out of Mount Zion. The zeal of the Lord of hosts will perform this."

Isaiah 37:33 "Therefore thus says the Lord concerning the king of Assyria: He shall not come into this city or shoot an arrow here or come before it with shield or cast up a siege mound against it."

Isaiah 37:34 "By the way that he came, by the same way he shall return, and he shall not come into this city, says the Lord."

Isaiah 37:35 "For I will defend this city to save it, for My own sake and for the sake of My servant David."

Isaiah 37:36 "And the Angel of the Lord went forth, and slew 185,000 in the camp of the Assyrians; and when [the living] arose early in the morning, behold, all these were dead bodies. [II Kings 19:35.]"

Isaiah 37:37 "So Sennacherib king of Assyria departed and returned and dwelt at Nineveh."

Isaiah 37:38 "And as he was worshiping in the house of Nisroch his god, Adrammelech and Sharezer his sons killed him with the sword, and they escaped into the land of Armenia or Ararat. And Esarhaddon his son reigned in his stead."

Prayer pushes the spirit of fear away, and gives you freedom according to Psalms 118:5-6. Psalm 118:5 "Out of my distress I called upon the Lord; the Lord answered me and set me free and in a large place."

Psalm 118:6 "The Lord is on my side; I will not fear. What can man do to me? [Heb. 13:6.]"

Prayer will build you up in your soul according to psalms 138:3. Psalms 138:3 "In the day when I called, You answered me; and You strengthened me with strength (might and inflexibility to temptation) in my inner self.

When you live a life of prayer it will bring you guidance. Isaiah 58:9 -11 **"Then you shall call, and the Lord will answer; you shall cry, and He will say, Here I am. If you take away from your midst yokes of oppression [wherever you find them], the finger pointed in scorn [toward the oppressed or the godly], and every form of false, harsh, unjust, and wicked speaking, [Exod. 3:14.]"**

Isaiah 58:10 **"And if you pour out that with which you sustain your own life for the hungry and satisfy the need of the afflicted, then shall your light rise in darkness, and your obscurity and gloom become like the noonday."**

Isaiah 58:11 **"And the Lord shall guide you continually and satisfy you in drought and in dry places and make strong your bones. And you shall be like a watered garden and like a spring of water whose waters fail not."**

When feeling a sense of harm or fear, prayer will remove that feeling of harm. Joel 2:32. **"And whoever shall call on the name of the Lord shall be delivered and saved, for in Mount Zion and in Jerusalem there shall be those who escape, as the Lord has said, and among the remnant [of survivors] shall be those whom the Lord calls. [Acts 2:17-21; Rom. 10:13.]"**

Prayer will also bring spiritual understanding. Colossians 1:9-12. **"For this reason we also, from the day we heard of it, have not ceased to pray and make [special] request for you, [asking] that you may be filled with the full (deep and clear) knowledge of His will in all spiritual wisdom [in comprehensive insight into the ways and purposes of God] and in understanding and discernment of spiritual things–"**

Colossians 1:10 **"That you may walk (live and conduct yourselves) in a manner worthy of the Lord, fully pleasing to Him and desiring to please Him in all things, bearing fruit in every good work and steadily growing and increasing in and by the knowledge of God [with fuller, deeper, and clearer insight, acquaintance, and recognition]."**

Colossians 1:11 **"[We pray] that you may be invigorated and strengthened with all power according to the might of His glory, [to exercise] every kind of endurance and patience (perseverance and forbearance) with joy,"**

Colossians 1:12 **"Giving thanks to the Father, Who has qualified and made us fit to share the portion which is the inheritance of the saints (God's holy people) in the Light.'**

Prayer will help you to be filled with the fruit of righteousness according to Philippians 1:9-11.

Philippians 1:9 **"And this I pray: that your love may abound yet more and more and extend to its fullest development in knowledge and all keen insight [that your love may display itself in greater depth of acquaintance and more comprehensive discernment],"**

Philippians 1:10 **"So that you may surely learn to sense what is vital, and approve and prize what is excellent and of real value [recognizing the highest and the best, and distinguishing the moral differences], and that you may be untainted and pure and unerring and blameless [so that with hearts sincere and certain and unsullied, you may approach] the day of Christ [not stumbling nor causing others to stumble]."**

Philippians 1:11 **"May you abound in and be filled with the fruits of righteousness (of right standing with God and right doing) which come through Jesus Christ (the Anointed One), to the honor and praise of God [that His glory may be both manifested and recognized]."**

Prayer helps you to live a peaceful life. Bringing peace to your mind, body and spirit. 1 Timothy 2:1-2.

1 Timothy 2:1 **"FIRST OF all, then, I admonish and urge that petitions, prayers, intercessions, and thanksgivings be offered on behalf of all men,"**

1 Timothy 2:2 **"For kings and all who are in positions of authority or high responsibility, that [outwardly] we may pass a quiet and undisturbed life [and inwardly] a peaceable one in all godliness and reverence and seriousness in every way."**

Prayer strengthens your relationship with God. 2 Thessalonians 3:5.

2 Thessalonians 3:5 **"May the Lord direct your hearts into [realizing and showing] the love of God and into the steadfastness and patience of Christ and in waiting for His return."**

Prayer brings forth fruitfulness Colossians 1:9-12.

Colossians 1:9 **"For this reason we also, from the day we heard of it, have not ceased to pray and make [special] request for you, [asking] that you may be filled with the full** (deep and clear) knowledge of His will in all spiritual wisdom [in comprehensive insight into the ways and purposes of God] and in understanding and discernment of spiritual things–"

Colossians 1:10 "That you may walk (live and conduct yourselves) in a manner worthy of the Lord, fully pleasing to Him and desiring to please Him in all things, bearing fruit in every good work and steadily growing and increasing in and by the knowledge of God [with fuller, deeper, and clearer insight, acquaintance, and recognition]."

Colossians 1:11 "["We pray] that you may be invigorated and strengthened with all power according to the might of His glory, [to exercise] every kind of endurance and patience (perseverance and forbearance) with joy,"

Colossians 1:12 "Giving thanks to the Father, Who has qualified and made us fit to share the portion which is the inheritance of the saints (God's holy people) in the Light."

Prayer gives us a full knowledge of Christ's love. Eph 3:16-19.

Ephesians 3:16 **"May He grant you out of the rich treasury of His glory to be strengthened and reinforced with mighty power in the inner man by the [Holy] Spirit [Himself indwelling your innermost being and personality]."**

Ephesians 3:17 **"May Christ through your faith [actually] dwell (settle down, abide, make His permanent home) in your hearts! May you be rooted deep in love and founded securely on love,"**

Ephesians 3:18 **"That you may have the power and be strong to apprehend and grasp with all the saints [God's devoted people, the experience of that love] what is the breadth and length and height and depth [of it];"**

Ephesians 3:19 **"[That you may really come] to know [practically, through experience for yourselves] the love of Christ, which far surpasses mere knowledge [without experience]; that you may be filled [through all your being] unto all the fullness of God [may have the richest measure of the divine Presence, and become a body wholly filled and flooded with God Himself]"**

God Promises To Answer Our Prayer When We…

Isaiah 58:9 **"Then you shall call, and the Lord will answer; you shall cry, and He will say, Here I am. If you take away from your midst yokes of oppression [wherever you find them], the finger pointed in scorn [toward the oppressed or the godly], and every form of false, harsh, unjust, and wicked speaking, [Exod. 3:14.]"**

Isaiah 58:10 **"And if you pour out that with which you sustain your own life for the hungry and satisfy the need of the afflicted, then shall your light rise in darkness, and your obscurity and gloom become like the noonday."**

Having faith in God. Mark 11:22-24.

Mark 11:22 **"And Jesus, replying, said to them, Have faith in God [constantly]."**

Mark 11:23 **"Truly I tell you, whoever says to this mountain, Be lifted up and thrown into the sea! and does not doubt at all in his heart but believes that what he says will take place, it will be done for him."**

Mark 11:24 **"For this reason I am telling you, whatever you ask for in prayer, believe (trust and be confident) that it is granted to you, and you will [get it]."**

When we forgive others. Mark 11:25-26.

Mark 11:25 **"And whenever you stand praying, if you have anything against anyone, forgive him and let it drop (leave it, let it go), in order that your Father Who is in heaven may also forgive you your [own] failings and shortcomings and let them drop."**

Mark 11:26 **"But if you do not forgive, neither will your Father in heaven forgive your failings and shortcomings."**

When we Pray in the spirit. Ephesians 6:18.

Ephesians 6:18 **"Pray at all times (on every occasion, in every season) in the Spirit, with all [manner of] prayer and entreaty. To that end keep alert and watch with strong purpose and perseverance, interceding on behalf of all the saints (God's consecrated people)."**

When we pray according to God's will. 1 John 5:14.

1 John 5:14 **"And this is the confidence (the assurance, the privilege of boldness) which we have in Him: [we are sure] that if we ask anything (make any request) according to His will (in agreement with His own plan), He listens to and hears us."**

When we obey the Lord's commandments. 1 John 3:22.

1 John 3:22 **"And we receive from Him whatever we ask, because we [watchfully] obey His orders [observe His suggestions and injunctions, follow His plan for us] and [habitually] practice what is pleasing to Him."**

The Importance of Prayer

Will we do the greater things the Bible speaks about? Ephesians 1:16 -18.

Ephesians 1:16 **"I do not cease to give thanks for you, making mention of you in my prayers."**

Ephesians 1:17 **"[For I always pray to] the God of our Lord Jesus Christ, the Father of glory, that He may grant you a spirit of wisdom and revelation [of insight into mysteries and secrets] in the [deep and intimate] knowledge of Him,"**

Ephesians 1:18 **"By having the eyes of your heart flooded with light, so that you can know and understand the hope to which He has called you, and how rich is His glorious inheritance in the saints (His set-apart ones),"**

Luke 18:1 **"ALSO [Jesus] told them a parable to the effect that they ought always to pray and not to turn coward (faint, lose heart, and give up)."**

Prayer gives God the permission to act in agreement with His will.

Ephesians 6:18 **"Pray at all times (on every occasion, in every season) in the Spirit, with all [manner of] prayer and entreaty. To that end keep alert and watch with strong purpose and perseverance, interceding on behalf of all the saints (God's consecrated people)."**

Praying in the Spirit

Praying in the spirit is mentioned three times in the Bible. 1 Corinthians 14:15.

1 Corinthians 14:15 **"Then what am I to do? I will pray with my spirit [by the Holy Spirit that is within me], but I will also pray [intelligently] with my mind and understanding; I will sing with my spirit [by the Holy Spirit that is within me], but I will sing [intelligently] with my mind and understanding also."**

Jude 1:20 **"But you, beloved, build yourselves up [founded] on your most holy faith [make progress, rise like an edifice higher and higher], praying in the Holy Spirit;"**

Praying in the spirit is really praying under the leading of the Holy Spirit.

It is praying concerning the things that the Holy Spirit shows us to pray for.

Romans 8:26 tells us, 'Romans 8:26 **"So too the [Holy] Spirit comes to our aid and bears us up in our weakness; for we do not know what prayer to offer nor how to offer it worthily as we ought, but the Spirit Himself goes to meet our supplication and pleads in our behalf with unspeakable yearnings and groanings too deep for utterance."**

Prayer Watches

First prayer watch (6pm-9pm)

I believe this is a time of great meditation and deep reflection as you pray, allowing God to bring into your remembrance all of what has happened this day and what is His plans to counteract all that would have transpired.

Even though it is a time that most people are weary because of all that they have been through within the day, we must push pass the weight and focus on God and what He is saying.

Second watch (9pm-12am)

This is a watch when most people are tired and are already asleep. Much focusness and energy is needed to pray and cry out to the Lord without being distracted or falling asleep. It is especially important for persons at this time to pray God's protection over everything concerning them. Psalms 68:1

Psalms 68:1 **"I believe this is also a time to pray strong because this is a watch that is right before the midnight hour."** So an intense prayer is needed.

Third watch (12am-3am)

As a servant of the Lord, this is a time of night, prayer warriors, prophet's, intercessors and believers of the Most High God shouldn't be asleep. Especially if this is the prayer watch that God has assigned you to.

This is a very dark time in the realm of the spirit and in the natural.

Witches, warlocks and those engaged and employed by Satan are up planning the demise of others. This just like other watches, we must be strategic in prayer in hitting the bulls eye.

This is not a time to be unfocused, this is a time of war. As a warrior we must know what we plan to stop, interrupt, hijack, dismantle, annihilate, and take back from the enemy. We possess power over the enemy. Let's use all that we possess to the honor and glory of God.

Fourth watch (3am-6am)

Even though this is a hour that sweet sleep is upon us, we cannot afford to be sleeping if this is the prayer watch that God has assigned to you. This is the hour to gain grounds and territory over the enemy. Take back what was stolen and to take back what lies in the enemy hand.

This is the hour to break forth all that this day shall bring to you. Take authority of this day and declare what is needed according to the will of God for your life, family and ministry.

I believe this was the time that Jesus walked on water to help the disciples who were in the storm. Matthew 14:25-33.

Matthew 14:25 **"And in the fourth watch [between 3:00–6:00 a.m.] of the night, Jesus came to them, walking on the sea."**

Matthew 14:26 **"And when the disciples saw Him walking on the sea, they were terrified and said, It is a ghost! And they screamed out with fright."**

Matthew 14:27 **"But instantly He spoke to them, saying, Take courage! I AM! Stop being afraid! [Exod. 3:14.]"**

Matthew 14:28 **"And Peter answered Him, Lord, if it is You, command me to come to You on the water."**

Matthew 14:29 **"He said, Come! So Peter got out of the boat and walked on the water, and he came toward Jesus."**

Matthew 14:30 **"But when he perceived and felt the strong wind, he was frightened, and as he began to sink, he cried out, Lord, save me [from death]!"**

Matthew 14:31 **"Instantly Jesus reached out His hand and caught and held him, saying to him, O you of little faith, why did you doubt?"**

Matthew 14:32 **"And when they got into the boat, the wind ceased."**

Matthew 14:33 **"And those in the boat knelt and worshiped Him, saying, Truly You are the Son of God!"**

This watch I believe is a time to gain spiritual prosperity and to stop the devil plans concerning your blessings and favor that the Lord has for you.

Fifth watch (6am-9am)

This watch is a more refreshed, energized and enthusiastic watch, being the normal time for persons to arise. Fresh and full of energy. This watch is the time for the Holy Spirit to get us ready for service. Whatever lies ahead concerning ministry for you. If you have engagements to preach etc.

This is a good time to seek God on instructions concerning the service, what he would have you to preach, what type of spirit is in operation, whatever questions pertaining to the services of God.

The book of acts declares it was around the third hour of the day or 9am, when the Holy Spirit descended in the upper room to equip the one hundred and twenty disciples for service. Acts 2:15 **"For these men are not drunk, as you imagine, for it is [only] the third hour (about 9:00 a.m.) of the day;"**

Sixth watch (9am-12pm)

This is a time to put before God all of the assignments he has given you to do and what is needed to successfully carry out these projects.

I believe this was the time that the israelites got what was needed to build the tabernacle. Exodus 12:35-36.

Exodus 12:35 **"The Israelites did according to the word of Moses; and they [urgently] asked of the Egyptians jewels of silver and of gold, and clothing."**

Exodus 12:36 **"The Lord gave the people favor in the sight of the Egyptians, so that they gave them what they asked. And they stripped the Egyptians [of those things]."**

Seventh watch (12pm-3pm)

I believe that it was during this time Daniel always went home to pray.

This is a time to know for high destruction in the world. It is wise to pray concerning protection psalms 91.

Eighth watch (3pm-6pm)

Like every other prayer watch I believe that this is the hour of dying to self (what self wants) and rejoicing in the power of our Lord God. Praying concerning the manifestation of things promised.

The Different Names of God

El Shaddai

Lord God Almighty.

Jehovah Nigad

The Lord who predicts the future.

Jehovah Ahavah

God is love.

El Elyon

The Most High God.

Adonai

Lord, Master.

Yahweh

Lord ,Jehovah.

Jehovah Nissi

The Lord my banner.

Jehovah Raah

The Lord is my shepherd.

Jehovah Rapha

The Lord that heals.

Jehovah Shammah

The Lord is there.

Jehovah Tsidkenu

The Lord our righteousness.

Jehovah Mekoddishkem

The Lord who Sanctifies you.

El Olam

The Everlasting God.

Elohim

God.

Qanna

Jealous.

Jehovah Jireh

The Lord will provide.

Jehovah Shalom

The Lord of peace.

Jehovah Sabaoth

The Lord of host.

Jehovah Tsedek

The Lord of justice.

Jehovah Chesed

The Lord is merciful.

Jehovah Magen

The Lord a shield.

Jehovah Kadosh

The Lord is Holy, Pure, and Undefiled.

Jehovah Hayah

The Great I Am.

Jehovah Or

God is Light.

Jehovah Kavod

The Lord of Glory.

Spiritual Nugget

Psalm 63 A Psalm of David; when he was in the Wilderness of Judah.

Psalm 63:1 **"O GOD, You are my God, earnestly will I seek You; my inner self thirsts for You, my flesh longs and is faint for You, in a dry and weary land where no water is."**

Psalm 63:2 **"So I have looked upon You in the sanctuary to see Your power and Your glory."**

Psalm 63:3 **"Because Your loving-kindness is better than life, my lips shall praise You."**

Psalm 63:4 **"So will I bless You while I live; I will lift up my hands in Your name."**

Psalm 63:5 **"My whole being shall be satisfied as with marrow and fatness; and my mouth shall praise You with joyful lips"**

Psalm 63:6 **"When I remember You upon my bed and meditate on You in the night watches."**

Psalm 63:7 **"For You have been my help, and in the shadow of Your wings will I rejoice."**

Psalm 63:8 **"My whole being follows hard after You and clings closely to You; Your right hand upholds me."**

Psalm 63:9 **"But those who seek and demand my life to ruin and destroy it shall [themselves be destroyed and] go into the lower parts of the earth [into the underworld of the dead]."**

Psalm 63:10 **"They shall be given over to the power of the sword; they shall be a prey for foxes and jackals."**

Psalm 63:11 **"But the king shall rejoice in God; everyone who swears by Him [that is, who binds himself by God's authority, acknowledging His supremacy, and devoting himself to His glory and service alone; every such one] shall glory, for the mouths of those who speak lies shall be stopped."**

Hindrances from Answered Prayer

Weird heart (this is a people who have God in their mouths but not in their heart, he is the furthest thing from there spirit, these are the people that the Pastor has to tell when to pray, fast, read the word etc...) the scripture makes it clear. Isaiah 29:13.

Isaiah 29:13 **"And the Lord said, Forasmuch as this people draw near Me with their mouth and honor Me with their lips but remove their hearts and minds far from Me, and their fear and reverence for Me are a commandment of men that is learned by repetition [without any thought as to the meaning],"**

Disregard for others (these are a people with no love, compassion, regard, care or feelings for others. All that matters is about me myself and I.

No love for humanity. But the Lord wants us to be more like Him. To love as He loves, to give as He gives, to care as He cares. He has shown us by His example that it can be done. He shows the example for us to follow John 13:34. John 13:34 **"I give you a new commandment: that you should love one another. Just as I have loved you, so you too should love one another."**

Idols in our lives (the best definition of an idol is something we ourselves make into a god. It can be anything that stands between us and God, or something or someone that we substitute for God). Things that are sometimes taken as idols are leaders, vehicles, husbands, furniture, house etc.... Here is what scripture has to say. Ezekiel 14:3.

Ezekiel 14:3 **"Son of man, these men have set up their idols in their hearts and put the stumbling block of their iniquity and guilt before their faces; should I permit Myself to be inquired of at all by them?"**

Wrong motives (this is a set of people with the wrong intentions and hidden agendas. A people that possess hidden secrets. I was told that one may see a man but not what's in his heart, so you don't know what he is thinking and what's on the inside concerning you). The word of God says in James 4:3.

James 4:3 **"[Or] you do ask [God for them] and yet fail to receive, because you ask with wrong purpose and evil, selfish motives. Your intention is [when you get what you desire] to spend it in sensual pleasures."**

Waywardness, it is important to stay with God. You cannot have a part of you with God and a part of you will the devil. Be sold out for God and give Him all of you. Allow Him to order your steps and be obedient to follow His order. Jeremiah 14:10-12.

Jeremiah 14:10 **"[And the Lord replied to Jeremiah] Thus says the Lord to this people [Judah]: In the manner and to the degree already pointed out have they loved to wander; they have not restrained their feet. Therefore the Lord does not accept them; He will now [seriously] remember their iniquity and punish them for their sins."**

Jeremiah 14:11 **"The Lord said to me, Do not pray for this people for their good."**

Jeremiah 14:12 **"Though they fast, I will not hear their cry; and though they offer burnt offering and cereal offering [without heartfelt surrender to Me, or by offering it too late], I will not accept them. But I will consume them by the sword, by famine, and by pestilence."**

Refusal to hear God's word; Blocking out His word and the person that He uses to bring the word of God. Sometimes we can judge a person in such a way, because of what we see in the natural and miss God because of what He is doing in the spirit. We must be alert, and always remember to consult the Holy Spirit concerning the word of God and the works of God.

The word of God declares in Proverbs 28:9.

Proverbs 28:9 **"He who turns away his ear from hearing the law [of God and man], even his prayer is an abomination, hateful and revolting [to God]. [Ps. 66:18; 109:7; Prov. 15:8; Zech. 7:11.]"**

When you pray it shouldn't be from a place of anger. Genesis 21:17.

Genesis 21:17 **"And God heard the voice of the youth, and the angel of God called to Hagar out of heaven and said to her, what troubles you, Hagar? Fear not, for God has heard the voice of the youth where he is."**

When we look closely at this we realize that Hagar was so angry that the Lord heard the youth which was her son and not her.

Iniquity in my heart; this is where true repentance comes in, where we ask God to purge us and remove everything that is not of God. The word of God says in the book of Psalms 66:18.

Psalm 66:18 **"If I regard iniquity in my heart, the Lord will not hear me; [Prov. 15:29; 28:9; Isa. 1:15; John 9:31; James 4:3.]"**

Spiritual Nugget

Knowing the voice of God, will stop you from making mistakes and will lead you, give instructions and direction on the right path. Your prayers must come from a pure place, not a place of anger and hurt. Here we see that God heard the prayer of Hagar son, because he was pure before the Lord.

Genesis 21:12-17.

Genesis 21:12 **"God said to Abraham, Do not let it seem grievous and evil to you because of the youth and your bondwoman; in all that Sarah has said to you, do what she asks, for in Isaac shall your posterity be called. [Rom. 9:7.]"**

Genesis 21:13 **"And I will make a nation of the son of the bondwoman also, because he is your offspring."**

Genesis 21:14 **"So Abraham rose early in the morning and took bread and a bottle of water and gave them to Hagar, putting them on her shoulders, and he sent her and the youth away. And she wandered on [aimlessly] and lost her way in the wilderness of Beersheba."**

Genesis 21:15 **"When the water in the bottle was all gone, Hagar caused the youth to lie down under one of the shrubs."**

Genesis 21:16 **"Then she went and sat down opposite him a good way off, about a bowshot, for she said, Let me not see the death of the lad. And as she sat down opposite him, he lifted up his voice and wept and she raised her voice and wept."**

Genesis 21:17 **"And God heard the voice of the youth, and the angel of God called to Hagar out of heaven and said to her, What troubles you, Hagar? Fear not, for God has heard the voice of the youth where he is."**

Sin will move you away from God and keep you in a position of hiding. Not wanting to be a part of any church gathering or spiritual assembly. It stops you from meeting with God in prayer and doesn't give you a hunger for the word of God nor the things of God. It puts up walls in the spirit realm and speaks to you as being less than or not enough. This is the devils plan to make you feel a sense of not needing God.

If this is you, I encourage you to get up and start moving the way it used to be weeks, months and years ago. The Heavenly Father awaits you with arms wide open to accept you.

The Bible says it in Isaiah 59:2. Isaiah 59:2 **"But your iniquities have made a separation between you and your God, and your sins have hidden His face from you, so that He will not hear."**

When you pray to be seen or noticed by others. Matthew 6:5-6.

Matthew 6:5 **"Also when you pray, you must not be like the hypocrites, for they love to pray standing in the synagogues and on the corners of the streets, that they may be seen by people. Truly I tell you, they have their reward in full already."**

Matthew 6:6 **"But when you pray, go into your [most] private room, and, closing the door, pray to your Father, Who is in secret; and your Father, Who sees in secret, will reward you in the open."**

A lack of faith in God and what He has promises to do. Going through the motion of prayer but just because of what you were taught to believe by forefathers. Your faith, hope and trust is not in God. There is an attitude of gratitude and expectancy that we need when going before the Lord in prayer. In Hebrews 11:6.

Hebrews 11:6 **"But without faith it is impossible to please and be satisfactory to Him. For whoever would come near to God must [necessarily] believe that God exists and that He is the rewarder of those who earnestly and diligently seek Him [out]."**

Pride in tithing or even fasting, feeling as though the leaders or the church at large owes you or has an obligation or commitment to favor you above all. Because of your wealth and riches concerning the ability to fund areas in the church and to pay tithes and offering. Luke 18:11-14.

Luke 18:11 **"The Pharisee took his stand ostentatiously and began to pray thus before and with himself: God, I thank You that I am not like the rest of men–extortioners (robbers), swindlers [unrighteous in heart and life], adulterers–or even like this tax collector here."**

Luke 18:12 **"I fast twice a week; I give tithes of all that I gain."**

Luke 18:13 "But the tax collector, [merely] standing at a distance, would not even lift up his eyes to heaven, but kept striking his breast, saying, O God, be favorable (be gracious, be merciful) to me, the especially wicked sinner that I am!"

Luke 18:14 "I tell you, this man went down to his home justified (forgiven and made upright and in right standing with God), rather than the other man; for everyone who exalts himself will be humbled, but he who humbles himself will be exalted."

The prophet's prayer

Father, I bow before You asking You to purge me this day, asking You Lord to remove, gut out anything inside of me that isn't right. Every lying tongue, gossiping spirit, slanderous spirit, every form of rebellion, remove everything out of my ear gate, things that I have allowed into my hearing, things that I have allow myself to see that wasn't right, idol conversations, places I went that I wasn't supposed to go, putting my hands to partake of things I shouldn't.

Lord I repent, forgive me. For You are my God. I praise You this day just for being God. I praise You Heavenly Father for the dew of the morning and the sunset at evening. I praise You for life and life more abundantly. Father You mean the world to me, even though I disappoint You at times and fall short of Your glory.

Teach me Your ways that I may be more like You.

For You are the one true God and there is none like You, none can even compare. Don't take Your Holy Spirit from me or hide Your face from me. I need You Lord, more than words can express. Lord I bring my words, knowledge, intellect etc....before You and I ask with all sincerity of heart, mind and body that You give me the words to express my feelings towards You in a virtuous way that brings honor and glory to Your name. It's in Jesus Mighty Name I pray, Amen.

Spiritual Nugget

How do you ascend into the hills of the Lord?Clean hands and a pure heart.

Knowing the voice of God will stop you from making mistakes, will guide and help you to live a spirit filled life.

Declarations for a Repented Life

As I embrace this new season of a repented life, may my mind, body and spirit adhere to the will and purpose of God in order to excel and be positioned for the next move of God.

I declare that I will seek the Lord with my whole heart according to psalms 119:2. "Blessed (happy, fortunate, to be envied) are they who keep His testimonies, and who seek, inquire for and of Him and crave Him with the whole heart." I decree and declare that from this day forward, there will be no more drinking of alcoholic beverages, no more lies, cursing, slandering, cheating, sexual immorality, sins done secretly or publicly.

My position now is to be a solider in the army of the Lord, evangelizing, teaching, interceding and living a life of holiness according to the word of God in 2 Timothy 2:3-4, "Take [with me] your share of the hardships and suffering [which you are called to endure] as a good (first-class) soldier of Christ Jesus. No soldier when in service gets entangled in the enterprises of [civilian] life; his aim is to satisfy and please the one who enlisted him."

The Lord thy God will be king and ruler of my life. I shall overcome every trial, billow, storm, or persecution set before me sent by the enemy to stop, hinder or distract me. In the Mighty, Name of Jesus Christ I shall overcome. With fruits of the Holy spirit being evident in my life, the glory will be given unto God.

Made in the USA
Middletown, DE
18 January 2022